THE WAIT FOR YOUR VOICE

THE SILENCE WE CARRY

UJJWAL GEHLOT

GLOBAL DISTRIBUTION

ISBN 979-889544329-3

Cover and interior Design: Ujjwal Gehlot

For My Mother

*"To the women who waged wars for my soul, who sheltered me from life's storms, and nurtured my heart's deepest goal - **thank you Maa for being my eternal home"***

For My Love

"To the one who saw the poet in me, when i couldn't see it myself, who whispered 'write' when the world whispered 'give up'
*"Your love is the ink that fills my pen, the paper that holds my thoughts, and the voice that echoes through my verse - **thank you lovii for being my muse, my guiding light."***

UJJWAL GEHLOT

This book will touch our soul and bring us closer together!

<u>*To the one holding this book*</u>

As you turn these pages, i hope you find solace in the echoes of my heart. may these words be a gentle embrace, a comforting whisper, or a guiding light in the darkness.
These poems and quotes are fragments of my soul, shared with the hope that they will resonate with yours. may you find pieces of yourself within these lines, and may the remind you that you are not alone in your journey.
With every word, I've pored out my heart, vulnerable and true. may you receive it with an open heart, and may it inspire you to embrace your own emotions, to love deeply, and to live authentically.

Thanks for being part of this journey.
May our heart connect through the echoes of love, longing and hope.
with love and vulnerability
UJJWAL GEHLOT

<u>The Wait for Your Voice</u>

In silence, I wait for your sound
A whisper, a word, a voice unbound
The echoes of memories we've made
Haunt the emptiness, a hollow shade

My heart beats slow, my soul feels old
Longing to hear your voice, young and bold
The wait is long, the silence is wide
But in the stillness, I'll wait and reside

For in the quiet, I hear my heart
Beating with questions, torn apart
Searching for answers, night and day
For the sound of your voice, to guide the way

In dreams, I hear your gentle tone
A soft breeze whispering, "You are not alone"
But dawn awakens, and I'm left to face
The silence that waits, an empty space

Still, I'll hold on to the hope in my chest
That someday soon, your voice will find its nest
And in the waiting, I'll find my strength
To hold on to love, and never let go again.

<u>How should I make you realize that :</u>

- ∞ I have always ran and chased after you, wanting to walk with you to together and forever.

- ∞ Your smiling face gives me reason and hope to want you even more, no matter whether its on side.

- ∞ I have been only on you from the starting and this will continue by me forever, no matter what happens and whoever comes in my life.

- ∞ Your dark brown eyes feels and drives me magically into the river of honey directed from haven's depth and charm hit by sunlight.

- ∞ Your cheerful bright **dimpled smile** is enough to make my day happy that is exerted by your beautiful face.

And that's why I am not afraid of anyone in this world, and always wants to protect you at any cost, because I love you with all my heart and I will always love you…

The fact is,

Loving the person who doesn't loves you is just like hugging the cactus. The more your hug, the deeper its hurts.

And when I gazed at those eyes for the last time, I realized that they never looked at me the way I looked them.

One sided love always hurts
*But right now I'm on the edge of loving you even
if that hurts, shatters my heart into pieces,
I'm willing to get hurt.*

I once poured my heart into a love story, weaving a tale of forever with the one I cherished. I scripted a happily-ever-after, where our love would flourish, and we'd entwine our lives in matrimony. Convinced that our bond would forever be sealed, I believed the ending would remain unchanged. But fate had other plans. We parted ways, and with a single click, the entire narrative was erased. The memories we created, the love we shared, and the future we envisioned – all deleted. Yet, the ache in my heart remains, a poignant reminder that sometimes, even the most beautiful stories come to an end, leaving only longing and what-ifs in their wake.

*The irony is that people are ready to die for love,
yet they say it will hurt them in the end.*

Just one day if I could be with you
Just one day if I could hold your hand of my
fingers through.
The day I want to spend my time only to realize
how you gleamed my eyes to shine

We highlight the important things in books, but in life, we often forget to highlight the most important thing – our own happiness. We remember our pain, recall the last time we cried, but forget the last time we laughed. It's life; everything keeps changing. The ones we laughed with yesterday, we may cry for today. We're crying because we remembered the painful moment when we got detached, but we forgot the precious moments we spent with our love.

My love, don't mistake my persistence for force,

I'll wait for your heart to melt, of course,

In this life or at my dying breath,

My devotion will prove its endless depth.

I won't force you to love me again, to talk to me, to laugh with me, or to rekindle our bond. But I promise to keep trying every day, until my last breath, to prove the depth of my love for you. Please don't mistake my persistence for coercion. I'll give you all the time you need, and I'll wait patiently for the day when your heart might soften. If it's meant to be, our love will reignite, even if it's just a flicker of warmth on my dying day. My love, don't let my efforts be in vain – let your heart melt, either in this life or when I'm gone.

The weight of her absence is a burden I bear with every breath.

Once
She wept for my life, *and I rose from the ashes.*
But
now, her absence is the flame that burns me, and
I'm left to perish in the embers of our love.

Tethered souls, we can't seem to break free,

A bond so strong, it's a bittersweet symphony.

We're willing to hurt, to let each other go,

But our hearts refuse to detach, don't you know.

<u>A Borrowed Light</u>

In the depths of darkness, where shadows play,
You held my hand, and lit the way.
Your tears, a river, that flowed through the night,
Guiding me back, to the warmth of life's light.

With every breath, you whispered low,
*"**Fight, my love,** and let your spirit glow."*
And I rose, from the ashes of pain,
With your love, as my solace, my heart's refrain.

But now, you're gone, and I'm left to grieve,
In the silence, where our love used to breathe.
The memories of you, a bittersweet refrain,
Echoes of joy, and a love that remains.

Your absence, a flame, that bums me whole,
A slow and painful death, in the embers of our
soul
***I'm dying, dying,** in the memories of our past,*
Forever lost, in the shadows that will forever last.

Yet, I'll hold on, to the light you brought,
A borrowed radiance, that guided me through
the dark.
And though you're gone, your love remains,
A beacon in the night, that still sustain.

Unbroken Bond

In whispers of deceit, you turned away
A stranger's words, a misunderstanding's sway
Years have passed, yet my heart remains
Forever tied to yours, through joy and pains

Like a river's flow, our love will never cease
Through storms of doubt, it will find its release
For in its depths, a promise was made
A bond unbroken, a love that's not faded

I've reached for you, through silence and through
pain
My words, a bridge, to heal the hurt in vain
But still, you turn, and walk away
Leaving me to face another lonely day

Yet, I'll not falter, I'll not lose my way
For in my soul, our love will always sway
Like a flame, that flickers, yet never dies
It guides me on, through tears and sighs

Oh, my love, don't let the shadows deceive
Our bond is strong, our love will forever breathe
Through every test, through every strife
I'll stand by you, and be your life....

In this darkest night, I'll be your star
Forever shining, near and far

*My love, my heart, my everything is yours
Eternally yours, my love, my world, my queen, my
force.*

Echoes of Absence

Her departure left a canvas bare,
A vibrant tapestry, now faded, worn, and rare.
The colors of our love, once bold and bright,
Now muted, dulled, and shrouded in endless night.

The whispers of her laughter, silenced and still,
Haunting echoes that linger, against my will.
In every shadow, a memory resides,
A bittersweet reminder of love's demise.

Solitude's dark whispers, a lonely refrain,
Echo through my soul, a heart in vain.
The ghosts of love's past, a mournful sigh,
Longing to revive, what's lost, and say goodbye.

In this hollowed space, I search for peace,
A respite from the ache, a world to cease.
But like a phantom, her absence roams,
Forever etched, in the chambers of my heart's
home.

<u>Deadly peace</u>

In her eyes, a deadly peace resides,
Like honey straining from the hive, it abides
. My soul craves to retain this peaceful state,
Though my heart is filled with bloodshed, my
brain debates.

The fire within me burns, my bones reduced to
ash,
My eyes turn to stone, yet hope's spark still
flashes.
A comfort kiss, a love so true, I see in her gaze,
A deadly peace that beckons, despite the war's
haze.

The battle between heart and brain rages on,
Like sun-scorched earth, dry and cracked, yet still
I yearn.
To become a star, and end this strife,
For in her eyes, that deadly peace is my life.

Though elusive as water for a fish, I'll pay the
price,
For the peace I saw in her eyes, my heart's
sacrifice.

*In the tapestry of my existence, you were the
thread that wove me whole.
Yet, you chose to unravel, leaving me a frayed
and faded fragment, a soul forever incomplete, a
heart that beats with a hollow tone*

I gave up my life's breath for her smile, a sacrifice that
only true love can justify.

<u>To the 'Girls' who are the precious diamonds in our lives,</u>

we acknowledge your rarity and value. We understand that your sparkle can sometimes be dimmed by the weight of unshared struggles. Please know that we're willing to listen, to understand, and to support you through life's challenges. **We're ready to touch your feet, to apologize,** and to make amends when we falter. Our apologies are sincere, because your presence in our lives matters more than words can express. We're not perfect, but our commitment to you is unwavering. We promise to strive for empathy, to bridge the gaps in understanding, and to nurture our bond with trust, respect, and open communication. For in the beauty of your light, we find our own strength, and together, our love shines brighter."

Love is a risk, but loving someone who has hurt you is a guarantee of pain

WHAT YOU ARE TO ME ?

If I could give you one thing in life, I would surely give you the ability to see yourself through my vision and perspective...

Only then you would realize what you meaning holds upon my life and how special you are to me.. ITS BECAUSE...

You don't need a gown or dress to be a princess. You don't need a crown to be a queen.

BECAUSE

You are more than an average person

THE ONE WHO IS

A diamond surrounded by pearls and crystals...

And at last
'Forever' *was just a word on a page, a promise meant to be broken, a love letter turned into a farewell note.*

Promises You Made

A love letter once held my heart tight
A promise of forever, shining bright
But now, it's just a distant memory
A bittersweet reminder of what used to be

*She wrote '**never leave you**' with a smile so wide*
But forever came and went, and she stepped
aside
The ink faded, the words lost their might
Leaving me with just a shattered light

she said, we make mistakes, we forget
But I remember every word, every promise, every
regret
For in the end, it was just a game, a fleeting thrill
And I was left to pick up the pieces of a love that
stood still.

Don't give your heart to those who'll play
With its strings like a puppeteer's sway
They'll dance with joy, while you're in pain
And leave you shattered, like autumn's rain
Don't love those who've proven to be cold
Their hearts are ice, their love, a tale of old
They'll whisper sweet nothings in your ear
But their words are poison, their love, a snare
Protect your heart, it's a precious thing
Don't let it be a toy for those who'll sting
Learn to love yourself, to heal and mend
For in the end, that's the only love that will
transcend.

A heart that beats no more

For her happiness, I gave my all
My life's thread, I willingly let fall
A sacrifice that only love can see
A heart that beats no more, yet still loves thee

In the depths of my soul, a flame burned bright
A love so fierce, it consumed my life's light
I drowned in the ocean of her eyes
And in that drowning, I found a strange surprise

A sense of peace, a sense of release
A love that sacrificed its own breath to cease
For in her happiness, I found my own
A love that died, yet still lives on.

<u>A Love That Was Lost</u>

In the darkness of my mind, I lost my way
Depression's grip, a never-ending gray
I sought escape, a fatal sleep
But fate revived me, my heart to keep

But then came her words, a dagger to my soul
'I don't care if you live or die, you're no longer
whole'
A heart once broken, now shattered and cold
A love that was lost, forever to grow old

In that moment, I knew I had to rise
From the ashes of love, and open my eyes
To see that I deserved more, to live and thrive
To find a love that heals, and a heart that
survives.

Her words were the sweet poison that awakened me from a coma, but put my heart into a deeper sleep, forever scarred by the realization that **I was never loved.**

And finally I learned that:

"Promises are like ink on paper, easily erased by the tears of betrayal"

Unseen love

In the shadows of what could've been,
Where love's ghosts whisper unseen,
A bridge of respect, we never built,
Now lies in ruin, our hearts stilled.

I took your love for granted, blind to the pain,
Left you unseen, with emotions in vain,
But now I see, with eyes that understand,
The value of love, and the heart I disowned.

Time to make amends, to heal the heart's scar,
To rebuild trust, and love that's been marred,
To choose to see, to hear, to respect and adore,
The love we had, and the love we can restore.

In this reflection, I see what I've done,
A chance to redeem, to love anew, to begin.

After she left I realized :

Love is not just a feeling, but a choice to see, hear, and respect the heart of another; ***a choice I failed to make,*** *but one I'll carry with me forever.*

I saw my sister, meticulously marking important dates on her calendar - festivals, exam dates, and milestones. But when the day arrived, her plans would often go awry. Similarly, we mark imaginary dates in our minds, hoping against hope for a specific outcome - the day they'll return, the day they'll forgive us, the day they'll shower us with love. But alas, we're left waiting for a date that doesn't exist on any calendar, a plan doomed to fail from the start.

In the conflict between heart and mind, love was the ceasefire I couldn't negotiate

You knew I was a puzzle incomplete without you, yet
you chose to leave, *taking the missing piece with you,*
and now I'm left with a hollow heart, forever unfinished.

*You say you yearn to talk, yet **I see no effort from your side.***
My heart has been calling out your name for so long,
But why does this cry remain unheard, a silent, mournful sigh?

After a long time, I finally mustered the courage to call her, hoping against hope that we could still fix things. But the response was a harsh wake-up call: 'The Number you are trying is unreachable'. Those words cut deep, hitting me like a ton of bricks. I realized, with a sinking heart, that I was too late. She had moved on, found happiness without me, and didn't even need me anymore. The thought was suffocating, a painful reminder that sometimes, people move on, and we're left to pick up the pieces of our shattered dreams.

Once My heart said ,

"The most daunting challenge lies not in moving on, but in erasing the memories that we made love stay."

Love's absence casts a shadow that darkness cannot claim, for in its depths, a heart's true light is lost, forever shrouded in the silence of what could have been.

We had a glimmer of hope when she unblocked me, and our conversations flowed effortlessly for two days. I thought we were on the path to healing and reconciliation. But then, without warning, she blocked me again. The shock was debilitating, and my heart felt like it was bleeding all over again. I'm back to square one, confused and unsure of what's going on. The brief taste of happiness only made the subsequent pain more unbearable. I'm torn between waiting for her to come around and moving on. Will everything work out in the end, or am I just setting myself up for more heartache?

You've claimed me as yours, but in doing so, I've lost myself. How can I reclaim my heart when it's already yours? **I'm trapped in the depths of your love**, *a prisoner of my own emotions. Forever yours, yet lost forever.*

<u>A Fragment of You</u>

In the tapestry of my soul,
You were the thread that made me whole.
A delicate weave, a intricate design,
Without you, I'm a frayed and faded line.

Your absence is a canvas unframed,
A work of art unfinished, a heart that's maimed.
The colors of our love, once vibrant and bright,
Now muted, dull, and shrouded in endless night.

In the gallery of my life,
You were the masterpiece that cut through strife.
But now, your absence is a hollowed space,
A echo of memories, a haunting, ghostly trace.

I'm a poem unfinished, a song unsung,
A melody that falters, a harmony that's wrong.
Without you, my heart beats with a hollow tone,
A soul that weeps, a love that's overthrown.

In the fragments of my heart,
I'll hold on to the pieces we once were from the
start
Though you're gone, your memory remains,
A bittersweet reminder of love's sweet pains.

Lost Autonomy

Your claim on me, a weight that I bear
A heart that's no longer mine, a soul that's
ensnared
In the depths of your love, I'm lost and confined
A prisoner of emotions, forever intertwined
How can I reclaim my heart, my identity?
When you've taken ownership, and set my soul
free?

I'm trapped in this love, a captive of my own
A heart that beats for you, a love that's
overthrown

I'll try to express the pain, the anguish and the
strife
But words fail me, as I'm lost in the depths of
your life.

Rainy Remembrance

In twilight skies, dark clouds convene,
A somber mood, a heart that's seen,
The first raindrop falls, a memory awakes,
A longing stirs, a heart that aches.

With every drop, a thought of you descends,
A bittersweet reminder of love that ends,
The rain-soaked streets, a reflection of my soul,
A melancholy echo, a heart that's lost control.

In this downpour, I'm drenched in memories,
A nostalgic ache, a longing that reverberates,
For a love that's lost, a heart that's astray,
A rainy remembrance, that's here to stay.

The rain clears, the clouds depart,
But your memory lingers, a lingering heart,
For in the rain, our love was reborn,
A fleeting dream, a moment that's sworn.

Shattered Trust

In the shadows of memories, I find
A heart once full, now left behind
The ache of abandonment, a pain so true
But deeper still, a wound shines through

For trust, once broken, cannot be made whole
A bond so fragile, lost to an other's soul
The weight of betrayal, a burden to bear
A heart once open, now locked in despair

In the silence, I hear a whisper low
Of promises broken, and vows that went slow
The ghosts of what we had, they linger near
A bittersweet reminder of joy and fear

Trust, once shattered, cannot be regained
A loss so profound, it cannot be explained.

It's not the abandonment that hurts, but the fact
*That **you shattered my faith, for an other's***
***sake,** so tact.*

My paradise?

Finding you once more, is my heart's last call
Where love is fulfilled, is my paradise after all.

Just as one healthy snack like an apple can't guarantee a lifetime of good health, your hurtful words and actions can't keep me away from you. Your aggression, rudeness, and curses are like mere Band-Aids on the deep wounds of our relationship. It seems only something as final as my own demise could sever the ties that bind me to you. My love for you is that unyielding, that resilient, and that doomed.

Just one answer my heart want,

If departure was inevitable, why take me in?
And if love was absent, why masquerade with kin?

<u>Shadows of Deceit</u>

In the labyrinth of your eyes, I saw a lie,
A promise of forever, a heart's goodbye.
You wove a tapestry of deceit and pain,
And I, a thread, was tangled in your game.

Why did you serenade me with tender words,
Only to silence me with a heart of birds?
Why did you paint a canvas of love and light,
If darkness was the truth, the endless night?

Unheard

In the quiet, I spoke a thousand words
A language of silence, a heart that's blurred
I screamed in whispers, a deafening sound
But you never listened, never turned around

My silence was a canvas, a work of art
A story of love, a shattered heart
But you never saw it, never heard the pain
And now I'm left with just a whisper, a refrain

In the quiet, I conveyed it all
But you never tuned in, never heard my call

In the silence, I search for a way,
To heal the rift, to bring back the day,
When love was whole, and hearts were light,
But now, only shadows take flight.

In the end, *she chose to walk the solitary path,
Shattering my dreams, like a fallen, shattered
math.
For even love's strong fortress, can be breached
and worn, Leaving me with sorrow's dark, and a
heart that's forlorn.*

Threads of trust unraveled, love's tapestry worn
Leaving shattered space, a heart that's moved on
Yearning to restore, to love once more
But love's light has faded, leaving shadows galore

<u>A Heart Torn Asunder</u>

*Hearts once entwined, now lie apart
Like shattered glass, a shattered heart
Love's warmth withers, like autumn's fade
Leaving sorrow's dark, and a heart betrayed*

*Tender threads of love, so intricately designed
Rent apart, like a tapestry left behind
Whispers of what could have been, echo through
time*

*A bittersweet reminder, of love's fragile rhyme
Even love's strong fortress, can be breached and
worn
Leaving scars that never heal, and a heart that's
forlorn
For love, like life, is fleeting and brief
A moment's beauty, lost in time's relief*

*In this hollow shrine, I search for what's past
A love that's lost, forever to last
Yet, even in sorrow, love's memory stays
A bittersweet reminder, of love's fleeting ways.*

Behind the Mask

A shattered heart, a smile so wide,
A paradox that leaves the world outside,
Wondering how, I still manage to thrive,
In this dark place, where love has died.

My lips curve high, a masquerade so fine,
Concealing pain, a heart that's lost its shine,
The world sees joy, but I feel only strife,
A life undone, a soul that's lost its life.

I dance in the shadows, with steps so light,
A macabre waltz, through the dark of night,
I'm alive, yet dead, in this endless space,
A haunting enigma, a flickering pace.

My smile, a shield, that guards my heart's pain,
A protection from the world's prying gaze, in vain,
For in its depths, a storm forever rages,
A heart, once whole, now shattered, like fallen
pages.

A smile, a masquerade, conceals my pain
A heart, once whole, now shattered, like fallen rain
Yet, I persist, in this endless night
A haunting enigma, a flickering light.

Though I was angry, their love was in sight
If I was upset, they should have made it right
I admitted my mistake, and asked them to stay
But before leaving, they should have claimed me
as theirs, in every way.

What was meant to be, has come to pass
Yet, in the process, I've lost what truly mattered
at last
My heart, once full of laughter, now weeps with
pain
For in loving, I've lost myself, like summer's
fleeting rain

Darling!
In the ink of my words, tears are shed
A heart's cry, in every line, is said
If they reach you, and your heart beats as mine
Then, **take them in your arms***, and let our*
hearts entwine

*Once my grandpa told me
"Speak not so profoundly, that they forget their
own sound."*

Share with Care

In the realm of words, a delicate dance
Where sharing too much, can take a chance
On the other's heart, and their own voice too
Leaving them silent, with nothing to pursue

Don't reveal so much, that they forget their way
Lest they lose their own, in the words you say
For in the silence, they must find their own sound
And in the stillness, their heart's true voice be found

So share your words, but share them with care
Lest the other person, forgets their own voice is rare

<u>Whispers of a Fading Ember</u>

In twilight's hush, where shadows softly fall
A love's lament echoes, a heart's final call
The whispers of anger, a fleeting, fatal spark
Extinguished the flame, that once lit the dark

In sorrow's hollow, a lonely silence reigns
A longing to be claimed, by love's sweet, tender
refrains
The ghosts of what's lost, in memories forever
stay
Echoes of a love, that faded away

In the ashes of what could have been, a whisper
remains
A love that was worth fighting for, in heart's
deepest pains
Yet, the embers of longing, forever will smolder
and gleam
A bittersweet reminder, of love's ethereal dream.

Its hard for heart to accept but mind said..

"No resentment, just a simple truth
Their heart's loyalty, no longer belongs to me, in
youth."

Babe!!

_Your eyes still whisper **'I love you'**, a language all their own,
But your words and actions say **'let go'**, and leave me to alone.
Why do you hold back, when your heart still feels the same?
Why do you deny our love, and **play this painful game?**_

In our love, a contrast so stark,
I sacrificed all, to leave my mark,
While they concealed me from prying eyes,
A love so strong, yet hidden from the skies

Faith in love has withered, like a lost refrain,
The visions we crafted, now reduced to pain,
Don't hope for me to love once more, *for I'm undone,*
The nomad heart in me, has lost its way, and moved on.

She once asked me, "why do you refer to my family as your?"
I couldn't reply that time, but after she left me my heart whispered:

When I loved you, I didn't just embrace you, I adopted your family as my own. I gave them my heart, my respect, and my loyalty. But in the end, you took away not just our love, but **the family we had built together.**
You left me with a hollowed heart, a home that's no longer whole, and a sense of belonging that's lost forever.

I fought to stay afloat, but destiny didn't care,
Abandoned by those I loved, with no one to repair.
The hands that once held mine, now pushed me away,
In the depths of despair, I'm left to face the gray

My lips may smile, but my eyes betray,
The pain I hide, in a heart that's Grey.
My smile's a mask, that conceals my sorrow,
But my eyes reveal, the depth of my tomorrow

You're not in my life, yet you're its very soul,
A love that makes me whole, makes me complete,
makes me new.
In your absence, I find a strange, sweet refrain,
A heart that beats for you, in love's sweet pain

Yesterday, you said I was yours and you were mine.
But today, I'm struggling to connect with you,
even though we're in the same room. It's hard to
understand why things changed so fast

Eyes that shine but never dim, are like a love that's never known,
The beauty of heartache, the joy of making it home.
And what is love, if it doesn't have its share,
Of laughter and of tears, of joy and of despair?

Smiling eyes without tears, are love's incomplete sigh,
True love's story is unfinished, without a tear to dry.

Just like a smoker who can't resist the lure of nicotine despite the glaring warning labels, I find myself hopelessly addicted to loving you. Even after the harsh lessons and painful scars you've left me with, my heart refuses to quit. It's as if I'm drawn to the flame, knowing it will burn me again, yet unable to resist its warmth. Your love is my nicotine, my poison and my passion, a toxic allure that I cannot shake off. And so, I'll continue to love you, despite the danger signs, despite the hurt, despite the cautionary tales my heart keeps telling me.

Love's cruel fate, we can't escape,
Loving deeply means losing, an inevitable ache.
Today's delight will turn to tomorrow's tears,
For the one we hold closest, will bring us the most
fears.

Surrounded by shadows, I pen down my pain,
Tears of longing, like monsoon rains, forever
remain.

Dark clouds gathered, and I thought of you,
The first raindrop fell, and memories shone through.
I got drenched, and your memory soaked me too,
But alas, you didn't return, even for a moment,
anew

Comprehend my heartache, and smile with glee,
Relieve me of this anguish, and set my soul free.

<u>Lost in the shadows</u>

In the depths of their heart, a change took place
A shift in loyalty, a different pace
No anger or rage, just a quiet sway
Away from me, and what we used to say

Their heart's devotion, like autumn leaves
Fell away, and no longer breathes
The loyalty we had, now lost in time
Leaving me with just this hollow rhyme

Memories linger, like whispers in the night
Echoes of what we had, a fading light
I reach for what's left, but it slips away
Like sand between fingers, at the end of each day

In their eyes, a distance now resides
A space where love once lived, now hides
Their heart's loyalty, a fleeting dream
Lost in the shadows, where love's light no longer
beams.

Tears of Sorrow

If you understand my heart's deep pain,
Laugh and let go, like summer's driving rain,
Take away this anguish, this weight I bear,
And leave me with tears, my only solace there.

In your comprehension, I find a peaceful place,
A smile that heals, a warm and gentle space,
So grasp my grief, and laugh with joyful sound,
And take away this sorrow, that's weighed me
down.

With every tear, a memory fades away,
A bittersweet reminder of love's fleeting stay,
Yet in your understanding, I find a peaceful shore,
Where tears of sorrow, become tears of

Echoes of a Faded Vow

In whispers of what could have been,
A promise lingered, now unseen,
Two hearts once beat as one,
In love's sweet harmony, now undone.

Entwined in arms, we vowed to stay,
Through life's tempests, come what may,
But fate, like autumn's leaves, did stray,
And swept our love away.

Memories of joy, now taunt my mind,
A bittersweet reminder of what's left behind,
Tears fall like rain, a sorrowful refrain,
Longing for love's warmth, now but a fading
strain.

In this hollowed space, I search for peace,
A respite from heartache's ceaseless release,
And though it's hard to let go, I must confess,
Our love was but a fleeting caress.

Yet, in dreams, I still hear your gentle voice,
A whispered promise, a heartfelt choice,
To love forever, through life's joys and fears,
Now, but a haunting echo, through all my tears.

Together forever, was the vow we both made,
In each other's arms, the world's noise was faded.
Now, to soothe my crying heart, I tell myself,
Perhaps separation was our fate, not their
betrayal or wealth.

Maybe the most important chapter she can help you write, is the one where you learn to close the book on what's past, and open your heart to the stories yet to come.

Just as iron sharpens iron, your harshness is unexpectedly honing my love for you. With each cutting word, each rough edge, I find myself falling deeper under your spell. Your rudeness is tempering my heart, strengthening my devotion, and refining my passion. Like a paradoxical alchemy, your hurtful words are transforming into a strange, unyielding love that only grows more resilient with each blow.

In the void of your absence, I search for my shore,
Where memories of you once dwelled, now lies a
hollow core.
My heart, once a refuge for your love, now stands
bare,
Longing for the thirst of your affection, that once
was my solace, my care.

<u>*Your heart needs to hear this:*</u>

It's okay to miss the one you love,
To feel the ache, sent from above.
Let your heart process the emotions that roam,
And know that with time, **the pain will find its**
home.

Life is a fragile fabric, woven with threads of love, loss,
and longing. Every strand is a story, every tear a
testament to the beauty of our shared humanity.

Unwritten Chapters

Our story ended, before its time
Leaving unwritten chapters, and unspoken lines
I'm still holding on, to the pages of our past
While she's writing new ones, that will forever
last

I yearn to learn, from her courageous heart
To find the strength, to play a brand new part
To discover the beauty, in unwritten scenes
And the freedom that comes, with closing old
dreams

Threads of Connection

We are threads in the tapestry of life
Interwoven stories, a delicate strife
Each strand unique, yet bound together
Forming a fabric of love, weathered and tender

In the frays and tears, our scars are shown
But still, we hold on, to what makes us whole
For in the threads of connection, we find
A beauty that's stronger, than the tears we leave
behind

<u>*The love we shared*</u>

*In the depths of her heart, I was the haven where
love resided
A sanctuary of joy, where laughter never
subsided
Her happiest refuge, her peaceful nest
Where dreams were woven, and memories found
rest*

*But now, I'm just a forgotten place
A memory lost in the labyrinth of time and space
She forgot the way to my soul's gentle shore
And left me with a heart that's grown old, forever
more*

*In the silence, I still hear her whispered sigh
A distant echo, a lingering goodbye
The shadows of love that we once knew
Haunt me, like a bittersweet, eternal rue*

*Yet, I hold on to the memories we crafted with
care
The laughter, the tears, the love we shared
For in the end, it's not the forgetting that cuts
deep.....*

*But the remembering of what we once were, in
love's sweet sleep
So let me remain, a forgotten address*

A memory of love, in her heart's secret recess
For even in oblivion, our love will stay
A bittersweet reminder, of what could never fade
away

In the twilight of forgotten dreams
Our love will whisper secrets, in the silent
streams
And though she may forget, my heart will always
know
The love we shared, in the depths of her soul.

My heart yearns to reach you

You are the moon, I loved you like the sun
Longing to warm your gentle light, my day's just
begun
I see you rising every dawn's embrace
Yet, we remain apart, in this vast, empty space

Your soft beams illuminate the night's dark shore
My heart yearns to reach you, forever more
But like the sun and moon, we're bound to our
place
Never to meet, in this celestial pace

Still, I'll love you like the sun, with all my might
Warming your gentle light, in the dark of night
And though we're apart, my love will forever
shine
A constant heart, that beats in rhyme with thine.

<u>In Your Love, A Plant Took Root</u>

In the garden of my heart, I sowed a seed
A symbol of our love, a dream to proceed
The first leaf unfurled, and you appeared by my
side
Together we nurtured it, our love to abide
I saved that leaf, a token of our love's birth
Watered the plant daily, with tears of hope on
this earth

I envisioned us sitting, beneath its shade so wide,
A haven of love, where our hearts could reside
But like autumn's wind, you left, and I was alone
The plant remained, a reminder of what wed
sown.
Yet still, I tend to it, with love and gentle care,
For in its growth, I see our love still lingering
there.

Perhaps someday, you'll return, and we'll sit as
one,
Beneath the tree's embrace, where our love has
been sown.
Until then, I'll keep the plant alive,
A beacon of hope, our love will thrive and survive·

<u>Love's Efforts, Her Smile's Bliss</u>

Love is a journey of tireless devotion,
A path of endless efforts, a heart's emotion.
But then, her smile appears, like a radiant sun,
Illuminating all, and making the journey fun.

Her smile is a masterpiece, a work of art,
A symphony of joy, that reaches the heart.
It's a gentle breeze, that soothes the soul,
A warm embrace, that makes love whole.

In her smile, I find my peaceful nest,
A haven of happiness, where love finds rest.
For love may be a labor, of dedication and might,
But her smile is the reward, that makes
everything right.

So let me bask in the glory, of her lovely grin,
And let my heart be filled, with the joy that pours
within.
For love's efforts are worth it, for her smile's
sweet delight,
Is the treasure that makes, my heart take flight.

<u>Moonlit Longing</u>

I was alone, lost in love's embrace,
I grasped a wooden spoon, a whimsical pace.
I decided to converse with the moon's gentle face,
But night's dark clouds hid it from my eager gaze.

'Don't hide me!" I cried, 'Don't hide me!' the moon
and stars seemed to say,
Their voices loud, yet gentle as a summer breeze.
I thought the clouds were shielding them from
the rain's sweet sway,
But the moon implored the clouds once more,
'Don't hide me, please!"

The scene was surreal, yet I realized the earth
was parched and dry,
As I wondered, the first raindrop fell, a tear from
the sky.

It matched the one that fell from my eye,
a symphony of sorrow and sighs.
The rain poured down,
yet I sat, hoping the clouds would part,
And soon,
I'll find myself conversing with the moon, in all its
gentle art.

Read gently, lest I shatter like fragile glass,
For in your hands, my heart beats its last.
Though you own my soul, don't crush my every
part,
Lest I lose myself, and fade into the dark

Alone we enter this world, alone we depart. But in the silence of solitude, we discover the beauty of being alone.

Remember,
 healing is a journey, and it's okay to take your
time.
Be gentle with yourself, and trust that
you'll emerge stronger, wiser, and more radiant
than before.

The truth is that sometimes love isn't enough to keep people together. Its okay to feel the pain of her departure

*When I close my eyes I always see those eyes and
my heart kept aching,
So I wanted to forget it but ended up falling for
you again.
I cant escape, so please hold me.*

*Why my heart sinking?
It is because you live deep inside in my heart? Or
is it that I want you to truly stay with me?*

I was the ocean, you wanted rivers; I shone like the moon, but you sought statistics. We were two worlds, colliding in mismatched harmony.

Although my life's book is incomplete yet,
Life after you is a chapter I never wanted to
write.

I can't move on because
Every step forward feels like a step away from
our memories.

The faint light was turned off, but my eyes are lighting up again because of you as it feels like I would love you ages like this and pulled towards something that's in you,

And its not something, its someone
And that someone is you!
Yes, you my love!

Let's restart as,
Every day is a chance to rewrite the story of your
heart.

The world keeps spinning, but my heart still feels stuck to you and your memories.

Though love requires endless effort, her smile is a radiant reward that makes it all worthwhile.

In the cartography of her heart, I was once the place she called home, but now I'm just a forgotten coordinate, erased from her mind.

You are my moon, and I am your sun forever bound, yet forever apart. In this cosmic dance, we sway to the rhythm of love, our hearts entwined in a gravitational pull that transcends time and space.

In the hollow of her leaving, I find a silence that screams, a heart that mourns, and memories that haunt.

As you navigate the labyrinth of love, remember that pain and comfort are two sides of the same coin. There will be days when the heart aches, and tears fall like rain. But there will also be days when smiles bloom, and laughter echoes.

Don't let the pain define you, nor the comfort make you complacent. For in the depths of love's turmoil lies a truth: if destiny brought you together, it's because you're meant to be.

So, when the road ahead seems uncertain, and the heart feels heavy, don't give up. Make every possible effort to rekindle the flame, to revive the love that once was

For in the end, it's not the absence of pain that makes love worth fighting for, but the presence of comfort that makes it worth living for.

May the words on these pages be a reminder that you are not alone, and that your story is worth telling.
*If you liked the book please share your feedback to the author **@ujjwalgehlot01** or **@wordsofujjwal_** on Instagram. He'd love to hear you.*

THE WAIT FOR YOUR VOICE

UJJWAL GEHLOT